The world has enough for every man's need, but not enough for every man's greed.

Mohandas Karamchand Gandhi

VANISHING PEOPLES
YANOMAMI
PEOPLE OF THE AMAZON

BY DAVID M. SCHWARTZ
PHOTOGRAPHS BY VICTOR ENGLEBERT

LOTHROP, LEE & SHEPARD BOOKS   NEW YORK

Between the Mountains of the Wind and the River of Rains, where Brazil meets Venezuela deep in the Amazon rain forest, the world is green as far as the eye can see. In the midst of the foliage, a brownish ring of dried palm leaves pokes out of a clearing. It is the roof of the *yano*, an enormous doughnut-shaped hut made of poles cut from the forest and lashed together with vines, then thatched with leaves. Here, far from any city or town, the loudest noise is the screeching of parrots, and the brightest points of light are the iridescent blue wings of the morpho butterfly.

More than twenty families of Yanomami Indians live together inside the yano, side by side in a big circle of hearths. They sleep in hammocks hung in triangles around campfires that burn day and night. Wooden racks hold bananas and other fruits. Baskets, cooking utensils, and a few tools hang from the wall. The people have no other possessions. In the middle of the yano is the great plaza, open to the sky, where children play and their parents hold celebrations. The yano is an entire village under one roof.

5

In this village, called Batari-teri, ten-year-old Matuwe awakens to the soft hoots—"hrrroo, hrrroo"—of the *hutumi* bird. His sister Hiyomi is still asleep and the sun's rays have not yet sifted through the treetops to warm the yano, but his parents and baby brother are already awake. Like the other women, Wishami, his mother, bakes flatbreads over the coals. His father, Kaomawe, hunches beside the fire, sharpening a piece of bone to make an arrowhead.

Matuwe drops from his hammock and stoops beside Kaomawe. He too must learn to make arrows from the raw materials of the forest: a straight piece of cane for the shaft, a grooved hardwood plug for the butt, cotton fibers to hold the two together, plumes from the black curassow to help the arrow fly straight. While Matuwe watches, his father presses the arrowhead into the six-foot shaft. It fits tightly and Kaomawe is pleased. Later he will coat the arrowhead with poisonous resin from the bark of the virola tree. Shot into a monkey, the resin will paralyze the animal, and in minutes it will fall from its perch.

8

Kaomawe gathers his arrows and his seven-foot longbow, and he leaves with three other men. Barefoot, they file through the trees. On a good day they will return with a giant anteater or tapir, or perhaps an armadillo or monkey. Or they may come home empty-handed.

9

After a breakfast of flatbreads, Matuwe and other boys of the yano set out on their own kind of hunt. Armed with bows and arrows, they stalk lizards, frogs, birds, rodents—no small creature is safe! The younger boys usually miss their targets, but older ones such as Matuwe and his friend Rikomi are expert archers. Standing motionless for many minutes, they wait until their quarry comes within range.

Zzzzzzat! Twirling and whistling, an arrow flies through the air. It finds its target. Matuwe has killed a lizard, his fifth of the day. Rikomi has shot four. They cook their kill over small fires in the yano, but the lizards will not be eaten. To boys, hunting and cooking are just for fun.

Irara **This honey-loving member of the stoat (weasel) family has a nasty skunklike smell.**

While the men hunt, a large party of women and children go off in search of termite nests, big brown globes plastered to the sides of trees. The nests contain thousands of winged black termites and fat white grubs, or larvae, which are bigger and more nutritious than the adult termites. They cut the nests in half, impale them on sticks, and tap them until the wingless grubs drop out onto leaf pouches placed beneath the nests. The grubs will be roasted at the family hearths. On some days, the gatherers pursue frogs, land crabs, or caterpillars, or they look for vines that can be woven into baskets.

When they return to the yano, Hiyomi and Wishami tackle another chore. Hiyomi peels the roots of a garden plant called manioc, while Wishami grates the root and presses out the juices through a basket held between her legs. Wishami then forms the paste into thick, flat cakes that must dry in the sun before they can be baked. Later Hiyomi makes smaller cakes to cook at a hearth the girls have set up to look just like a family's living area. The miniature cakes taste just as good as the big ones her mother makes! For both girls and boys, playing helps to perfect the skills they will need when they have families of their own.

15

In the middle of the day, a noisy throng of children gathers in the central plaza and heads for the river. One by one, the youngsters leap into the water from high branches on the bank. A few good-natured tussles break out, complete with splashing, hair pulling, and name calling, but soon the insults are forgotten and the pack of rambunctious children returns to the yano, where a new kind of fun begins. Matuwe pulls Riko-mi across the mud floor of the plaza on a giant palm leaf. Chirping wildly with laughter, everybody takes a turn. But for most children, the favorite game is "jaguars and prey." Half of them are the jaguars chasing their prey, while the others, pretending to be pursued by the big cats, shinny up the poles of the yano to escape. Then everyone switches parts.

The game lasts into the afternoon, when the boys and girls return to the families' hearths. They know they must gather more food before the sun drops to the treetops. Some children join their parents in a trip to the family garden; others go to a fishing hole in the river.

The people of Batari-teri are skilled gardeners. In a large garden plot with a section for each family, they cultivate bananas, sugarcane, mangoes, sweet potatoes, papaya, manioc, and many other crops. But no garden is permanent. To protect the thin soil, which can easily lose its fertility, the Yanomami gardeners move their plots frequently. Forest trees soon return to the former gardens, and the rain forest suffers no permanent harm.

This afternoon Wishami and the baby join a fishing party. On the way to the river, the group stops to cut the poisonous *ayori-toto* vine. Children help the men beat the vines with thick sticks until they separate into many fibers and the sap flows freely. The sap contains poisons strong enough to stun fish when the men sweep the vines through the water. Dazed, the fish rise to the surface. Wishami and the others quickly scoop them into baskets before the toxin wears off. *Ayori-toto* poison does not pollute the river because it quickly breaks down and loses its effect. Fish that have not been caught recover and swim away.

Women often carry 70- or 80-pound loads of manioc (*below*), cassava (*left*), or other produce.

Urucu pod **When the grains are pressed together, they form a greasy soaplike bar used for painting.**

Whether they are fishing, gardening, hunting, or sitting at their hearths, the Yanomami wear almost no clothing. Women wrap themselves with fringed aprons a few inches long; men wear only narrow waistbands tied to their penises. When they want to "dress up," the Yanomami paint one another with lines, spots, and squiggles. They use red dyes made from *urucu* seeds, purple dye from palm-fruit juice, and the jet black powder of charcoal, inscribing any design that strikes their fancy. For a finishing touch, many wear brilliant wing feathers from parrots and toucans and the long tail feathers of macaws, and boys deck their heads with soft white down from the breasts of hawks. Girls make armbands of scented leaves and necklaces of seeds. Many girls pierce their ears, noses, and lips to insert blossoms or slivers of wood. Decorated in this way, a young girl hopes to attract a man who will ask her father if he can marry her.

When Hiyomi was six years old, Kaomawe promised her in marriage to Yebiwe, who lives across the yano. Fathers betroth their daughters when the girls are very young, but these engagements rarely work out. Hiyomi visited Yebiwe for months, taking food her mother prepared. Every day they ate together and talked. But they never became friendly and eventually stopped seeing each other. So Kaomawe betrothed Hiyomi to another man, whom she likes better. If they still enjoy each other's company when Hiyomi begins to menstruate, she will hang her hammock next to his, and they will be married.

Tonight Hiyomi is not thinking about her future husband. When it is nearly dark, the four hunters emerge from the forest. Bringing up the rear, Kaomawe trudges into the yano, a giant anteater draped over his back. Matuwe and Hiyomi know that this means many tasty meals. Kaomawe and two other men cut the animal into pieces and distribute the meat around the yano. None will go to waste, for Yanomami hunters never kill more than the villagers can eat. Otherwise, they will be haunted by the vengeful spirits of the dead animals.

Kaomawe will not eat any meat from the anteater. Yanomami hunters believe the spirit of the quick and agile hawk guides them in the hunt, and they fear that the hawk spirit will abandon anyone who eats what he himself has killed. A successful hunter always offers his kill to others— his family, fellow hunters, tribesmen too old to hunt, anyone who is hungry. All people are equal, say the Yanomami, and all must eat. It is a great honor for the courageous hunter to share his kill. He can be confident that another hunter will be equally generous with him.

Sometimes game and crops are scarce near the yano, and the entire village must leave on a *wayumi*, a trek lasting many days or weeks. During the *wayumi*, the trekkers live mainly on roots that grow wild in the forest. When night falls, the men make crude bark hammocks by stripping a few trees and tying together the long ribbons of bark with knots at both ends. To keep dry, they lash some poles into a lean-to and cover them with broad leaves. As always, the Yanomami meet all of their needs with the bounty of the rain forest.

A *wayumi* is not necessary now because hunters can find game close to the yano, but Matuwe and Hiyomi look forward to a different kind of trek. Early in the rainy season, the next time the full moon rises over the great plaza, the peach palm fruits will be ripe. Then the people of Batari-teri will visit a large grove of *rasha* trees, peach palms, in an abandoned garden near a deserted yano.

The days pass and the moon grows full. The time has come! Nearly everyone leaves the yano on the overnight journey. It is a joyous outing, full of anticipation. With their bows and arrows, the young men walk in front, silently scanning the forest for game. Older men follow behind, with women and children bringing up the rear.

Finally they reach the peach palms, laden with red, orange, and yellow fruit. But the fruit is not easy to reach. The bunches are just below the crowns of the trees—forty feet off the ground—and razor-sharp spines ring the tree trunks! The villagers are not discouraged. Several men climb smooth-barked trees nearby and cautiously edge out on limbs to approach the spiny peach palms. From their perches, they tie vines into loops to lasso the fruit. After a few tries, the climbers snare their targets and tear them from the branches—except for one immense bunch that is just a little too high to reach.

A limber young man knows how to solve that problem. He climbs down and lashes four short poles into two X's, then ties the X's to the peach palm tree. Standing on one X while gripping the other in his hands, he pushes the other one up, then climbs onto it and pulls up the lower one. Little by little, the keen climber inches his way up the trunk, never touching its barbs.

The people on the ground scurry about, gathering fruit. Soon their baskets overflow, and women hoist them onto their backs. To hold the heavy loads in place, they use bark straps tied to the baskets and looped over their foreheads. The long walk back to the yano is slow, but the harvest has been handsome. Happy chatter fills the air. Everyone is talking about a feast.

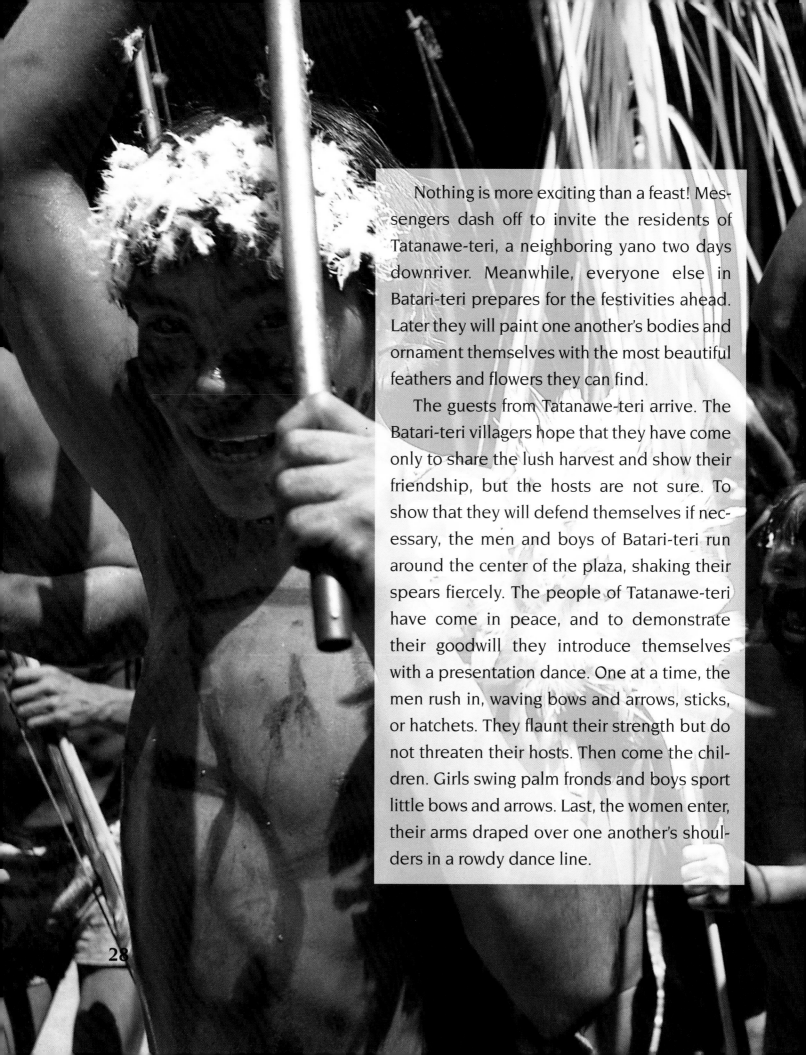

Nothing is more exciting than a feast! Messengers dash off to invite the residents of Tatanawe-teri, a neighboring yano two days downriver. Meanwhile, everyone else in Batari-teri prepares for the festivities ahead. Later they will paint one another's bodies and ornament themselves with the most beautiful feathers and flowers they can find.

The guests from Tatanawe-teri arrive. The Batari-teri villagers hope that they have come only to share the lush harvest and show their friendship, but the hosts are not sure. To show that they will defend themselves if necessary, the men and boys of Batari-teri run around the center of the plaza, shaking their spears fiercely. The people of Tatanawe-teri have come in peace, and to demonstrate their goodwill they introduce themselves with a presentation dance. One at a time, the men rush in, waving bows and arrows, sticks, or hatchets. They flaunt their strength but do not threaten their hosts. Then come the children. Girls swing palm fronds and boys sport little bows and arrows. Last, the women enter, their arms draped over one another's shoulders in a rowdy dance line.

28

The feathers for men's armbands are bound to small sticks with thread and beeswax.

Pretending to be a capuchin monkey, a man interrupts the dance. He hops about and makes monkey faces. The audience laughs wildly.

When the dance ends, it's time for a serious meeting, and the men of the yanos gather for a news talk. They exchange information about births, deaths, marriages, and feasts. Then the discussion turns somber. The Tatanawe-teri tribesmen have distressing news: Farther downriver, *nabuh*—foreigners—have arrived. They have overrun the land like ants on ripe fruit. They dig up the ground and the riverbank, turning the water an ugly shade of brown. The fish downriver are gone. The *nabuh* also cut many trees.

The Tatanawe-teri villagers have heard that the *nabuh* carry loud sticks that kill animals, and now there are places where almost no game is left. Without meat, the Yanomami who live in these places go hungry. N*abuh* have even shot at Yanomami children who tried to hide in the trees. As they fell, the *nabuh* shouted, "Monkeys!" And some people say that whole yanos have been ambushed, everyone murdered.

The men of Batari-teri listen attentively as the Tatanawe-teri villagers continue. Many Yanomami living near the *nabuh* have fallen sick. They die from strange diseases no one has seen before—diseases that the shamans and the helping spirits cannot cure.

The terrible story frightens the Batari-teri tribesmen. They fear that their great strength and keen weapons will not be enough to defeat the *nabuh*. But no one from Tatanawe-teri has ever seen these *nabuh*. Maybe they will not come to Tatanawe-teri or Batari-teri. Maybe the stories are not even true. Maybe there are no *nabuh*.

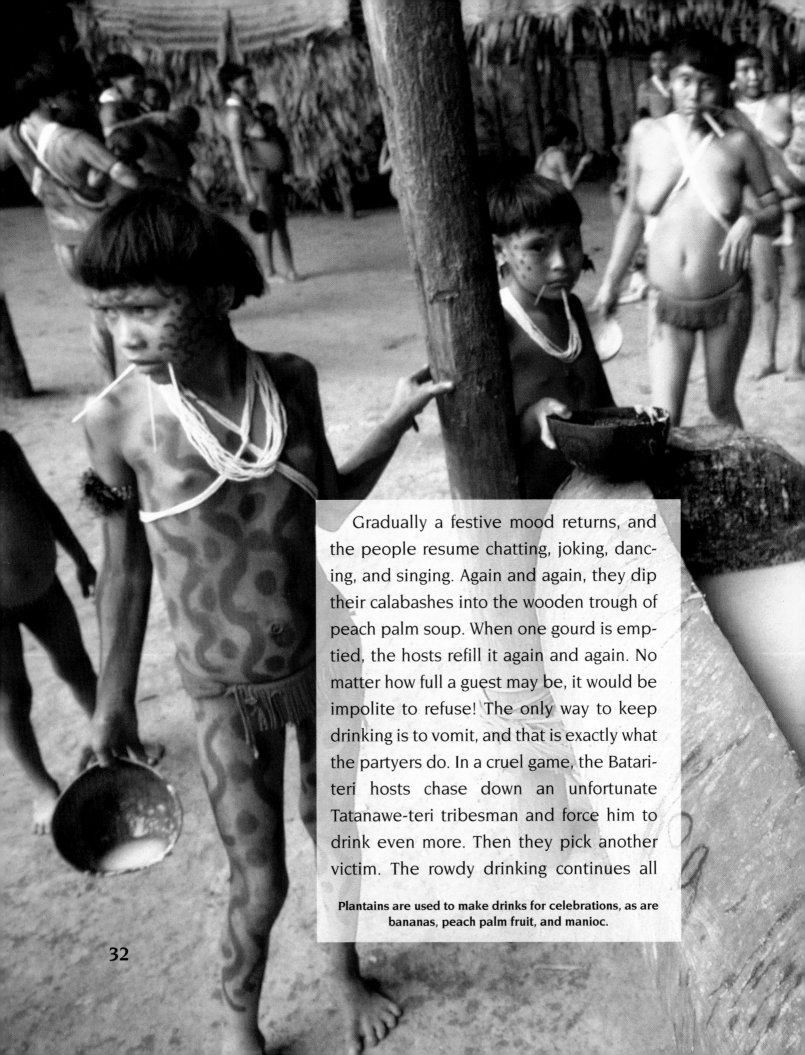

Gradually a festive mood returns, and the people resume chatting, joking, dancing, and singing. Again and again, they dip their calabashes into the wooden trough of peach palm soup. When one gourd is emptied, the hosts refill it again and again. No matter how full a guest may be, it would be impolite to refuse! The only way to keep drinking is to vomit, and that is exactly what the partyers do. In a cruel game, the Batari-teri hosts chase down an unfortunate Tatanawe-teri tribesman and force him to drink even more. Then they pick another victim. The rowdy drinking continues all

Plantains are used to make drinks for celebrations, as are bananas, peach palm fruit, and manioc.

Weaving liana strands into baskets (*above*), pounding manioc to make soup (*upper right*), and making new thatch for the roof (*lower right*).

Before the guests leave in the morning, they want to trade household goods with their hosts. They can offer many valuable items they received in trades with other yanos. An ax and several fishhooks are exchanged for fine bows and arrows, an aluminum cooking pot is traded for clay plates, a machete for several gourds of dye. The traders haggle loudly, sometimes angrily, but eventually everyone is satisfied. Then the visitors depart. Life in Batari-teri returns to its usual routine.

35

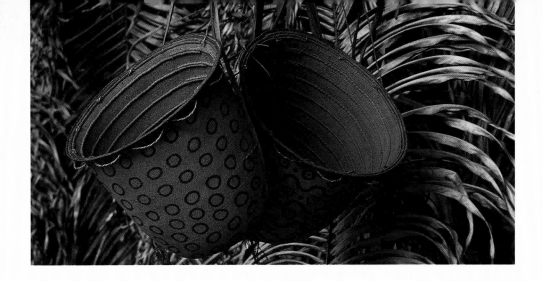

A few weeks later, the people of Batari-teri plan another feast, but for a very different reason. An old woman has died. After weeping aloud and mourning the dead woman for a day, the villagers wrap her body tightly in a bundle of sticks. They hang it from a tree and let it decompose for several weeks. Then they lower the bundle, remove the skeleton, and drop it into a raging fire. The ashes are mixed into a soup, and the feast begins. Everyone drinks the soup to ensure that the woman's spirit will live on. All traces of her must be removed from the yano or her spirit will be angry. Her possessions are burned, her garden is cut down, and the floor of her hearth is raked clean. No one will ever mention her name again.

In the world of the Yanomami, all living things possess powerful spirits, or *hekura*, that can help or harm them. The *hekura* live in yanos in the sky, but they frequently leave their yanos and circle down to earth. Not only plants and animals but rain, night, moon, sun, and the forces of nature have *hekura* that can cure disease and bring success in the hunt. Or they can cause illness and terrible misfortune. To rid the yano of hostile spirits and to encourage friendly ones, the Yanomami must speak to the *hekura*. Only a shaman, or medicine man, can communicate directly with them.

A man smeared with mud to look like a pig at a funeral feast.

Squirrel monkey 14 species of monkeys live in Yanomami territory, and babies often become pets if their mothers are killed. Other favorite pets include parrots, macaws, agoutis, coatimundis, and peccaries.

Matuwe's friend falls ill the day after the funeral feast. His parents summon Horonami, one of the shamans of Batari-teri. He must speak to the *hekura* and request their aid in curing the child.

In order to contact the spirits, Horonami must inhale drugs made from virola-tree bark, seeds, or other plants. After drying the material over a fire, he grinds it to powder with two stones and asks someone to blow it into his nostrils through a long, hollow tube. When it hits his nose, the drug burns fiercely. He falls to the ground, dizzy and stunned. But Horonami is an experienced shaman and he is not frightened. He sits up and begins chanting to the spirits above, inviting them to visit.

Slowly Horonami goes into a trance. After a while he begins to hear voices and experience visions. "Moon spirit! Tapir spirit! Spirit of the *witi-witimi* bird! Come down to me!" he calls. For some time the shaman speaks to the *hekura*. Whenever he wants to call another spirit, he performs a dance and recites a special chant. To communicate with an animal spirit, he imitates the creature with cries and gestures. The spirits of fish, who live in cool waters, are asked to soothe the boy's fever. The monkey spirit, so nimble with its hands, is called to pluck germs from his body. The *hekura* tell Horonami which medicines will help cure his patient, and he ventures into the forest to find the right plants.

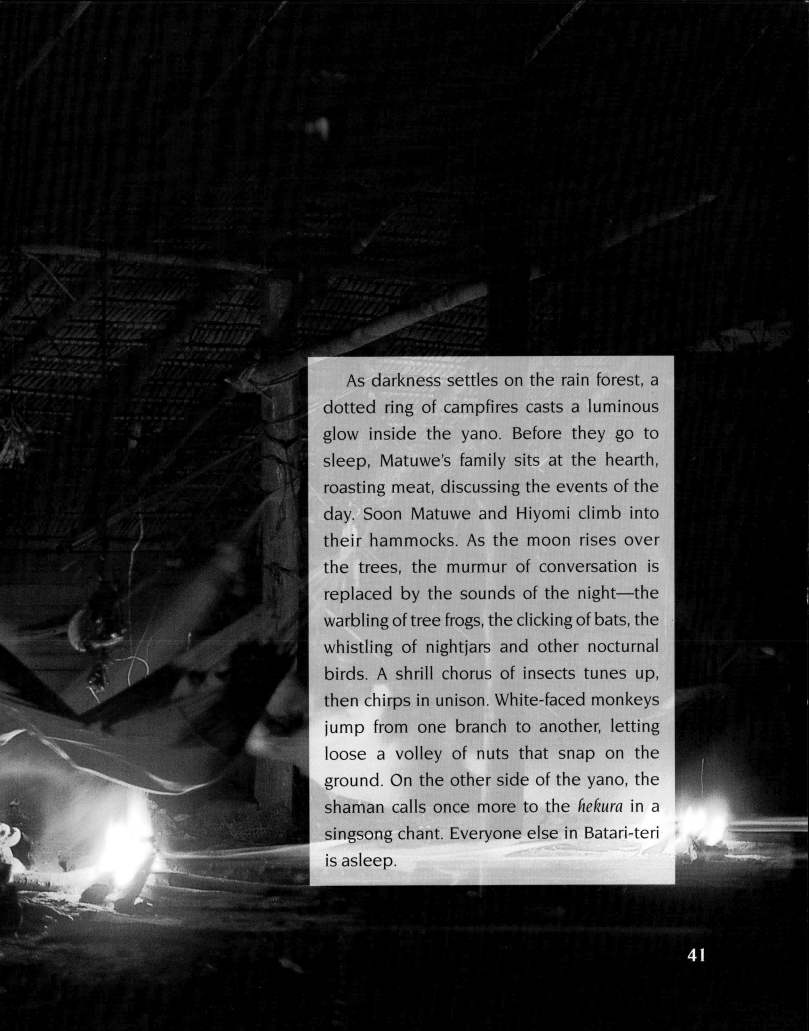

As darkness settles on the rain forest, a dotted ring of campfires casts a luminous glow inside the yano. Before they go to sleep, Matuwe's family sits at the hearth, roasting meat, discussing the events of the day. Soon Matuwe and Hiyomi climb into their hammocks. As the moon rises over the trees, the murmur of conversation is replaced by the sounds of the night—the warbling of tree frogs, the clicking of bats, the whistling of nightjars and other nocturnal birds. A shrill chorus of insects tunes up, then chirps in unison. White-faced monkeys jump from one branch to another, letting loose a volley of nuts that snap on the ground. On the other side of the yano, the shaman calls once more to the *hekura* in a singsong chant. Everyone else in Batari-teri is asleep.

LANDS OF THE YANOMAMI

MILES
0 — 300

KM
0 — 300

Caracas

Ciudad Bolivar

Orinoco River

VENEZUELA

GUYANA

COLOMBIA

YANOMAMI
TERRITORY

Boa Vista

Siapa River

BRAZIL

Rio Negro

Manaus

Amazon River

Transamazon Highway

Scarlet macaw Prized as a pet as well as for its colorful feathers.

Morning and evening, day and night, the rhythm of life in the yano has hardly changed for hundreds of generations. Now Matuwe and Hiyomi's generation may be the last to know the old Yanomami ways.

Like other tribal peoples around the world, the Yanomami are part of a complex, but delicate, web of life. To survive, they depend on the continued health of their environment—the plants, animals, water, soil, and air around them. Over many centuries, the rain-forest environment has been good to the Yanomami and the Yanomami have been good to the rain forest. Usually the fruits of the forest have been abundant. The people take what they need, but they leave behind much more than they take.

The Yanomami and other indigenous peoples of North and South America lived in peace with their environment for thousands of years. Then, five hundred years ago, Europeans began to arrive on American shores, altering and sometimes destroying the native peoples' lives and environments. Today the indigenous tribes of both continents suffer from the worst kinds of poverty, illness, and lack of education. They are among the most disadvantaged people on earth.

Isolation protected the Yanomami from these changes. Deep inside the world's largest jungle, they had very few visitors; while other indigenous groups were forever changed or died out completely, the Yanomami continued living as they always had. Now twenty thousand people strong, they are the largest tribe that lives by its ancient traditions. But motorboats and airplanes ended their seclusion, and the Yanomami are an endangered people.

Just a few years ago, miners began to descend in great numbers on the lands of indigenous tribes throughout the vast Amazon River basin of South America. The Amazon gold rush has brought wealth to a few lucky prospectors, but it has brought great sadness to many Yanomami. In many areas, thousands of gold miners, called *garimpeiros*, have overrun just a few hundred Yanomami. They have dug away at the riverbanks and clogged the waters with silt, using mercury to separate out the gold. Mercury pollutes rivers, kills fish, and poisons people who eat the fish that do survive. The prospectors have shot and scared away game, cut down trees, and trampled the land. They have brought malaria, tuberculosis, measles, flu, and other diseases the Yanomami never knew before—foreign illnesses that the shamans and the *hekura* cannot fight. Many miners have fallen ill or died from these diseases and the conditions the *garimpeiros* themselves have created. The

Yanomami are terrified. Nearly half of them now have malaria, and in some yanos, almost everyone has died. Other villages have lost all of their children and many of their elders. Entire yanos have been massacred. "Where the *garimpeiros* go," says the son of one Yanomami chief, "the Yanomami die."

Mining is not the only threat to South America's native peoples, and the Yanomami are not the only tribe that is endangered. Throughout the continent, governments build roads into tribal lands, encouraging people from the crowded cities to move there. Many indigenous people have lost their land to loggers, who clear vast tracts of forest to sell the timber. Forests that once teemed with life now stand barren. Soil washes off the land, clogging rivers that once ran clear, upsetting the web of aquatic life many miles downstream. Other lands have been taken over by ranchers who burn down the rain forest. Grass sprouts on the scorched earth, and for a few years cattle can browse amid blackened tree stumps. But before long, the soil loses its fertility and not even grass can grow. The ranchers move on, leveling another expanse of forest for their cattle. The havoc continues, a slow-motion wave of destruction. In a landscape that has lost its trees, the rains stop falling and a rain forest turns to desert.

Whether they dwell in the forest, the mountains, or the plains, the indigenous peoples of South America wish to live in harmony with their environment and in peace with the outside world. Yet, in many countries, they have no rights—even though their ancestors arrived in these lands a quarter million years ago.

Actual Yanomami life is very similar to what is described here, but Matuwe and his family don't exist and there are no villages called Batari-teri or Tatanawe-teri. These names represent many Yanomami and many yanos. To us, some customs may seem odd, unpleasant, or improper. Some may even shock us. Like people who are more familiar to us, at times the Yanomami are violent; they suffer hardship, disease, and sometimes hunger. The Yanomami are highly intelligent human beings who have mastered their environment. They are capable of deciding for themselves how they wish to live. Some have decided to join the modern world, but many would like to remain rooted in their land and their traditions. They are entitled to make that choice themselves.

Concerned people around the world have asked the governments of Brazil and Venezuela to protect the Yanomami, and in 1992 the two countries declared Yanomami land off-limits to everyone who is not part of the tribe. All the miners were ordered out, and many left. But time after time, promises to protect South America's indigenous peoples have been broken. Because the Yanomami are not allowed to own their land, the government of either country can, with a stroke of a pen, dissolve the protection it has offered. Will the governments continue to remove invaders so that the Yanomami can survive? Or will the Yanomami become extinct? No one knows. The Yanomami and other tribal peoples were the first people to live in the rain forest and the first to protect it. They have done so for thousands of years. Now, both the people and the rain forest itself could perish. Or the Yanomami could regain control of their destiny. If they do, both the rain forest and the Yanomami will survive.

Wildfowl such as curassows and guans resemble wild turkeys.

WHAT YOU CAN DO

You can help save the Yanomami and the Amazon rain forest. Here are some things you can do.

I. Educate Learn everything you can about the Yanomami and their current situation by keeping up with newspapers, magazines, and other literature published by organizations concerned with their survival. (Some of them are listed here.) Tell your family, classmates, friends, and neighbors about this tribe of endangered people and their struggle to survive. Help create an exhibit in your school or community and use it to raise both awareness and money.

II. Write Make your voice heard. Write to people who are in a position to help the Yanomami. Letters have an enormous impact on the decisions made by world leaders. A teacher or librarian can help you find the names of the current presidents of Brazil and Venezuela. You can address the letters as follows:

Presidente da República
Palacio do Planalto
Brasilia
70150.900 DF
Brazil

Presidente de la República
Palacio de Miraflores
Carmelitas
Caracas 1010
Venezuela

III. Contribute Join an organization that helps protect the Yanomami or contribute to a fund used to assist them. Money is needed to work with the Yanomami for emergency health care and to ensure that their rights are upheld and their lives safeguarded. Even small amounts of money can make a big difference. Try to multiply your contributions by asking other people in your school, family, or neighborhood to help.

These highly respected organizations accept United States funds and use them wisely for the benefit of the Yanomami and other tribal peoples. They also publish newsletters or magazines to inform contributors of important developments (good or bad) involving indigenous peoples.

Survival International is at the forefront of a worldwide movement to support tribal peoples. It believes in the right of indigenous peoples to decide their own future, and it helps them protect their lands, environment, and way of life. Since 1969 Survival International has campaigned with the Yanomami for recognition of their land rights, and in 1989 it opened an emergency health fund to raise money for vital health care. If you would like a free information packet or details on how you can join Young Survival and get involved with Survival International's campaigns, please write to:

>Young Survival
>Survival International
>310 Edgware Road
>London W2 1DY
>England

Cultural Survival is a human rights organization that works with native peoples and ethnic minorities around the world. It helps these people protect their homelands and support themselves economically through community projects that protect the environment and ensure their future. For further information, please write to:

>Cultural Survival, Inc.
>215 First Street
>Cambridge, MA 02142

Oxfam is an international development agency that helps people to help themselves. In Brazil, Oxfam works with Amazonian Indians and other forest dwellers to protect their land and their rights. Oxfam also assists slum dwellers, small farmers, agricultural laborers, and union workers in fighting for basic rights as employees and citizens. In all its projects, Oxfam recognizes that the health and welfare of people are linked to that of the environment; for this reason, the organization's projects include efforts to stop the destruction of the rain forest. Headquartered in England, Oxfam has an active U.S. office. For further information, write to either:

>Oxfam America   Oxfam
>115 Broadway   or   274 Banbury Road
>Boston, MA 02116   Oxford OX2 7DZ
>   England

Conservation International is dedicated to saving endangered rain forests worldwide and the numerous plants, animals, and indigenous peoples that rely on them for survival. Conservation International tries to balance conservation goals with local economic needs by providing financial and technical support to communities and local agencies. Conservation International works aggressively for the survival of indigenous peoples and the preservation of their rain-forest habitat. For information on membership, contact:

>Conservation International
>Suite 1000
>1015 Eighteenth Street NW
>Washington, DC 20036

To the Yanomami children
D.M.S.
V.E.

Many people helped create this account of the Yanomami and their precarious hold on survival. Fiona Watson of Survival International in London read my manuscript and offered useful suggestions. My agent, Regula Noetzli, knew exactly when to offer encouragement, advice, and support — and when not to. My editor, Judit Bodnar, was a font of good judgment and improved syntax. Finally, my friend and collaborator, Victor Englebert, allowed generous access to the wisdom and information he has gained from three decades of work with indigenous peoples around the world. —D.M.S.

Photographs by Mr. Englebert on pages 2–3, 25, 27, 31, 36, and 41 ©1982 Time-Life Books, from the "Peoples of the Wild" series, used by permission.

The display type was set in Bodega. The text was set in ITC Novarese Medium. Printed and bound by Tien Wah Press. Production supervision by Cliff Bryant. Map and illustration designed by Rodica Prato.

First Edition   1 2 3 4 5 6 7 8 9 10

Library of Congress Cataloging in Publication Data
Schwartz, David M. Yanomami: people of the Amazon / by David M. Schwartz; photographs by Victor Englebert.   p.   cm. ISBN 0-688-11157-2. — ISBN 0-688-11158-0 (lib. bdg.) I. Yanomamo Indians—Juvenile literature. [1. Yanomamo Indians. 2. Indians of South America—Amazon River Region.] I. Englebert, Victor, ill. II. Title. F2520.1.Y3S39 1994 981'.1004982—dc20 93-48616 CIP AC